TRUCKS!

By Lee Anne Martin

SCHOLASTIC

© 2010 becker&mayer! LLC

Published by Tangerine Press, an imprint of Scholastic Inc.
557 Broadway, New York, NY 10012
Scholastic Australia Pty. Ltd; Gosford NSW

Tangerine Press
an imprint of
SCHOLASTIC
www.scholastic.com

Produced by becker&mayer!, LLC.
11120 NE 33rd Place, Suite 101
Bellevue, WA 98004
www.beckermayer.com

If you have questions or comments about this product, please visit www.beckermayer.com/customerservice.html and click on the Customer Service Request Form.

Written by Lee Anne Martin
Edited by Delia Greve
Photo research by Zena Chew
Designed by Ryan Hobson
Design assistance by Rosanna Brockley
Production management by Larry Weiner

Printed, manufactured, and assembled in China
10 9 8 7 6 5 4 3 2 1
ISBN: 978-0-545-26300-9
09503

TRUCKS ARE MADE TO WORK!

They carry big, heavy loads, such as lumber, rocks, or even other trucks. They carry food, animals, cars, toys, gasoline. . . . Just about anything you can think of—a truck has probably hauled it from one place to another.

Trucks dig, push, lift, and load. They come in all sizes, from compact forklifts that buzz around warehouses to machines so huge they are as big as a building. Trucks help people in many ways. Fire trucks carry water to fight fires. Ambulances bring help in an emergency. When cars break down, tow trucks pull them out of sticky situations.

The biggest trucks have giant engines to haul a lot of weight. Smaller trucks are made to move easily through city streets to deliver bread from the bakery or mail to your home. There are so many different kinds of trucks from A to Z! How many have you seen? Turn the pages in this book—and see how many trucks you can name.

A

AIRPORT RESCUE TRUCK

These special fire trucks are used at airports to help in an emergency. They are so powerful they can spray water and firefighting foam as far as 210 feet (64 m). With all the nozzles open, this truck can spray 1,500 gallons (5,678 l) of water in a little more than a minute.

AMBULANCE

You have probably seen the flashing lights or heard the sirens of an ambulance as it zips by on its way to a hospital. Ambulances are stocked with medical equipment to take care of sick or injured people in an emergency.

AMPHIBIOUS TRUCK

This truck floats! It travels both on land and in water. The first widely used amphibious truck, called the DUKW (pronounced duck), was used to transport troops in World War II. Many of these amphibious trucks are now used to carry tourists around cities such as London, Boston, and Seattle.

ANTARCTIC TRANSPORTER

Antarctica is covered in snow and ice, which are tough to drive on. This vehicle was made to carry people around Antarctica. Huge balloon tires keep the truck from sinking in the snow and help it move over uneven ground.

ARMORED TRUCK

With an extra-strong metal covering, these trucks are made to protect. The police and the military use armored trucks to protect drivers and passengers. Private companies use armored trucks to carry money or other valuables from one place to another.

ASPHALT PAVER

These machines lay down a smooth layer of asphalt on the surface of a road or parking lot. Asphalt from the paver's hopper, or holding tank, moves down to the screed, a device that levels and shapes the asphalt on the ground.

AUTO TRANSPORTER

Also called a car carrier, this tractor trailer carries new cars to dealers where they will be sold. These transporters are about 70 feet (21 m) long and can hold about 12 small cars!

B

BACKHOE

Backhoes dig dirt, gravel, and concrete. A backhoe can dig holes, but it's especially good for digging ditches. Its long arm, or boom, pulls the backhoe's bucket through the earth, bringing up the dirt (or whatever it's digging) and leaving a hole behind.

BAGGAGE TRUCK

This little tractor helps at airports, pulling a train of carts filled with passengers' baggage. Before a plane takes off, the baggage truck moves the luggage from the terminal to the plane. After a plane lands, it collects the baggage from the plane and takes it to the terminal.

BILLBOARD TRUCK

These trucks travel around cities and towns pulling advertising billboards. They can be as small as an 8- by 10-foot (2.4- by 3-m) box truck, or as large as a semitractor-trailer. (See page 40.)

BOX TRUCK

A box truck is a rigid truck. That means the cab where the driver sits and the back of the truck don't move separately. Box trucks usually haul large items, such as furniture or appliances.

BRIDGE INSPECTOR TRUCK

This special type of bucket truck has a crane mounted in the back with a boom that can reach all the way under a bridge while the truck is parked on the deck. Workers in the bucket can look at the underside of a bridge to make sure it is safe.

BUCKET TRUCK

Also called a cherry picker, this truck has a bucket attached to a crane on the back. It carries people up in the air so they can work on things in high places, such as telephone wires. The bucket often has its own set of controls, so a worker can move it around. The name cherry picker comes from its original purpose, which was to help pickers reach fruit up high in trees.

BULLDOZER

This type of tractor has a large blade attached to the front for pushing sand, gravel, and dirt. (Pushing dirt is called dozing.) Bulldozers usually have tracks instead of wheels to help them move through heavy or wet dirt or sand.

C

CALFDOZER

This small bulldozer is often used to move dirt around for small jobs, such as landscaping and home repair.

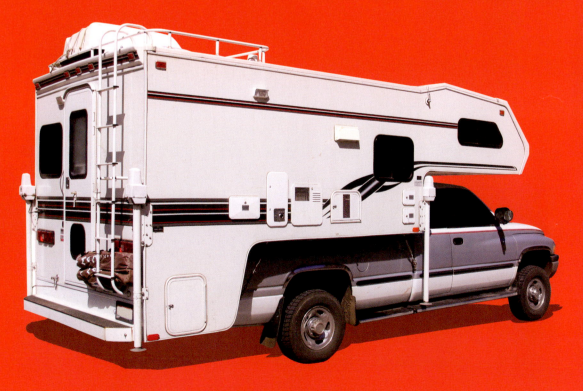

CAMPER

This is a pickup truck fitted with a shell that houses sleeping and eating areas, and even a tiny bathroom.

CATTLE CARRIER

This tractor trailer carries livestock, such as cattle, sheep, and pigs. The sides are slotted so the animals can breathe fresh air. Some carriers have two decks.

COMBINE

This machine harvests grain, such as wheat, oats, rye, or barley. It drives over a crop cutting the stalks, which are then fed into a thresher that separates the grain.

COMPACTOR

This large, heavy machine pushes down waste at a landfill. Its wide wheels are covered with sharp bumps that cut up the waste and give the machine traction.

CONCRETE MIXER

This truck both mixes and moves concrete. The drum, or mixer, on the back of the truck is loaded with dry materials, such as sand, gravel, or powdered cement, and water. Then the drum turns, mixing those materials together to make wet concrete. The truck drives to where the concrete is needed.

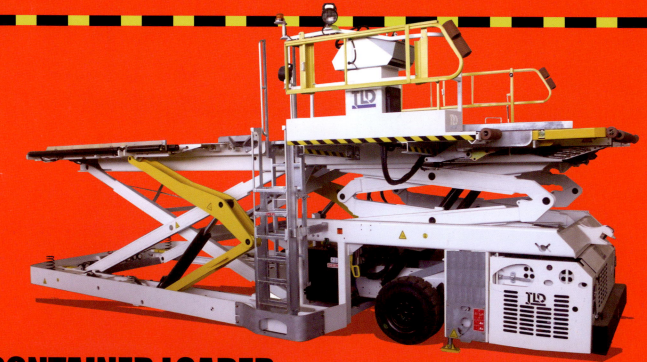

CONTAINER LOADER

This truck is a type of scissor truck used at an airport. Its large platform lifts cargo into the belly of the plane by opening and closing crossed supports like the blades of scissors.

CRANE TRUCK

The cranes on this truck, also called a boom truck, can lift and move heavy objects with a long arm, or boom. Some crane trucks can lift as much as 100 tons (91 tonnes)!

CURTAIN-SIDER

This tractor trailer has sides made of fabric, rather than hard sides like a box trailer. Because the curtains are simple to move, these trailers are easy to load but still protect the cargo from weather.

D

DE-ICING TRUCK

Used at airports, this truck has a telescoping boom—a long arm with joints that lengthen like the sections of a telescope. A worker sits in a bucket at the end of the boom to operate the nozzle. The truck sprays a liquid to melt ice from planes so they can fly.

DELIVERY TRUCK

Designed to carry laundry, milk, bakery items, flowers, packages, and other items, delivery trucks have been used since the 1920s. The driver's door slides open so he or she can hop in and out to make deliveries.

I OUBLE-DECKER TRAILER

This type of tractor trailer has two levels so it can hold even more cargo.

DRY BULK HAULER

These trucks can hold many kinds of dry materials, but often they carry grain. Grain is loaded into the bed of the truck from a hopper, or a tank, where it is stored. Then the hauler is ready to go!

DUMP TRUCKS

All dump trucks are used to carry sand, rock, and dirt from one place to another. There are many types of dump trucks, depending on how they unload material.

STANDARD DUMP TRUCK

Made to carry heavy loads of sand, rock, and dirt, a standard dump truck has an open box at the back. To dump its load, the front of the box lifts and the load slides off the back of the truck onto the ground.

ARTICULATED DUMP TRUCK

This type of dump truck is hinged together between the cab and the trailer, but the two sections cannot be separated. The hinge allows the truck to move over rough ground.

BOTTOM DUMP TRUCK

Sometimes called a belly dump truck, this type of dump truck has a gate on the bottom of its bin that opens to dump its load. Bottom dump trucks can spread an even path of gravel.

SIDE DUMP TRUCK

The box on this type of dump truck tilts sideways to dump its load, rather than back. This allows the truck to unload quickly.

TRANSFER DUMP TRUCK

Sometimes called a truck and pup, this is a standard dump truck that also pulls a separate trailer.

E EXCAVATORS

To excavate means to dig a hole. Excavators are vehicles made for digging up earth. Different types of excavators are made to dig in different ways.

XCAVATOR

Excavators look like giant backhoes. They are big machines used not only for digging but also to knock down buildings and other structures. They have a boom with a large bucket for digging and a cab that sits on a platform and can turn in any direction. An excavator can move on either tracks or wheels.

BUCKET-WHEEL EXCAVATOR

Among the biggest machines in the world, these earthmovers mine coal and other materials. A huge wheel with giant buckets on it pushes into the ground, scooping up coal. At 328 feet (100 m) tall and 656 feet (200 m) long, the machine is about as tall as a football field is wide and more than twice as long!

MINI EXCAVATOR

People use this lighter, more compact excavator for smaller digging jobs.

ROADHEADER

Used to dig tunnels, the roadheader's boom has one or more rotating spike-covered drums that break rock and dig into the earth as they spin. Roadheaders can tunnel about 20 feet (6.1 m) into the ground in an hour.

SUCTION EXCAVATOR

The pipe attached to the back of this type of excavator sucks up water, dirt, sand, and other materials and transfers them into the body of the truck. The hose reel on the front squirts water to clean sewer lines and other underground pipes.

TERRAIN LEVELER

This type of excavator has a large barrel attached to the front that is covered with sharp, curved teeth. When the barrel spins, it can cut into rock and create a level surface at the same time.

FIRE TRUCKS

There are many types of these special trucks, which are equipped to help firemen fight all kinds of fires.

HOOK-AND-LADDER FIRE TRUCK

Also called a tractor-drawn aerial, this type of fire truck is made to move through narrow city streets. These trucks have two steering wheels—one in the front and one in the back—to help them make tight turns. The truck's ladder can extend up to 100 feet (30 m) in the air (about ten stories), and the truck can pump about 1,000 gallons (3,785 l) of water in a minute.

ELEVATED PLATFORM FIRE TRUCK

This fire truck has a ladder that is hinged like an elbow, which allows it to go up and over obstacles such as buildings. Mounted on a turntable, the ladder can turn in any direction.

F

FIRE CHIEF'S TRUCK

The fire chief drives this truck to a fire. It carries electronic and communications equipment—everything the chief needs to lead the firefighters.

FLATBED TRUCK

This type of semitrailer has no sides or top. Flatbeds usually carry loads that won't be harmed by rain or snow, as well as things that are too large to fit in covered trailers, such as heavy machinery.

FORKLIFT

This truck gets its name from the two forks that stick out from the front. The forks are used to lift and carry objects too heavy for a person to pick up. Drivers often drive these vehicles backward because the loads the lifts carry in front make it hard for the driver to see.

FREEZER TRUCK

When frozen foods, such as meat, fish, ice cream, and ice, need to be moved, this rigid box truck with a freezer inside gets the job done.

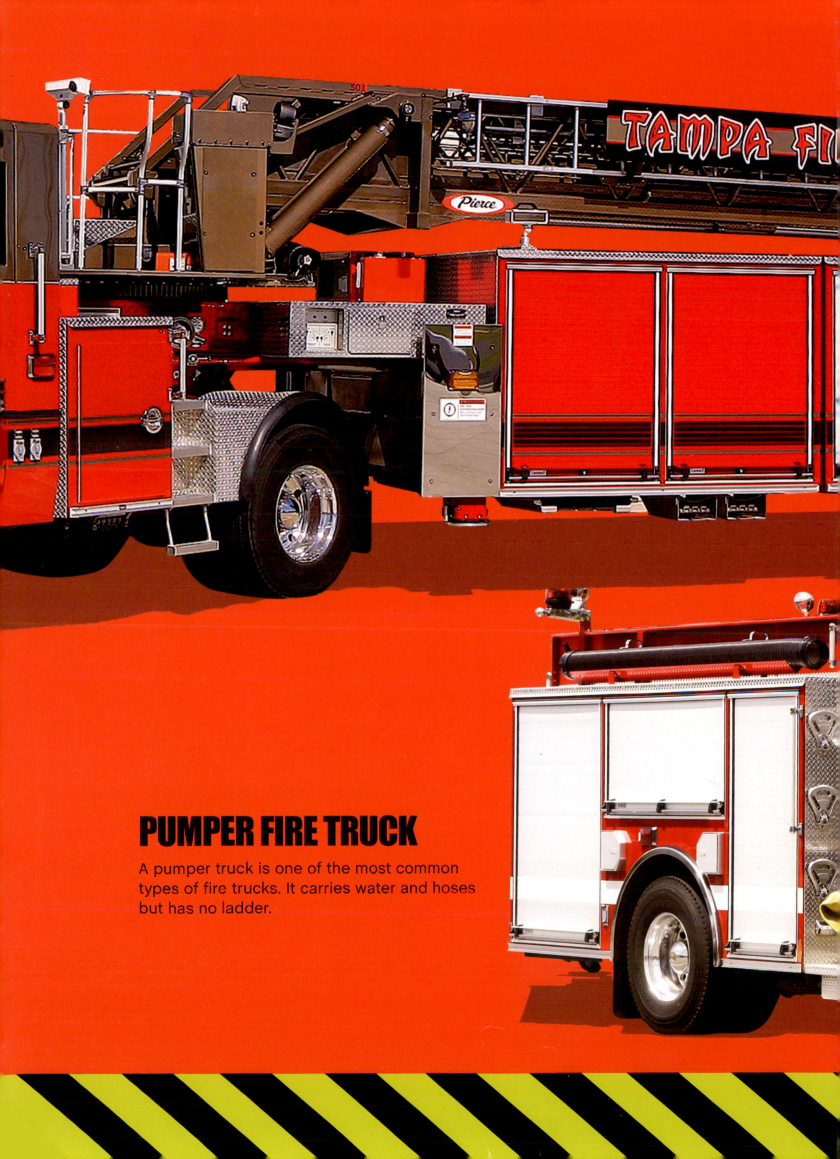

PUMPER FIRE TRUCK

A pumper truck is one of the most common types of fire trucks. It carries water and hoses but has no ladder.

BRUSH FIRE TRUCK

These trucks are designed to go off-road to fight fires in remote areas. They've got tanks, pumps, hoses, winches, special lighting, and a lot of space for storage.

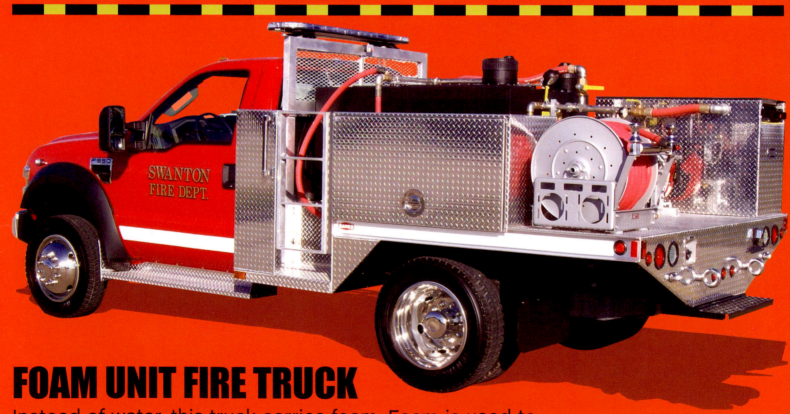

FOAM UNIT FIRE TRUCK

Instead of water, this truck carries foam. Foam is used to fight certain kinds of fires, including wildfires or fires caused by dangerous liquids.

HEAVY RESCUE FIRE TRUCK

This fire truck carries specialized equipment firemen may need to help people escape danger from a fire or another emergency.

TANKER FIRE TRUCK

These trucks can carry a lot of water—more than 1,000 gallons (3,785 l)! When there's a big fire where there are no fire hydrants, the tanker unloads its water into a special portable pool. Then the pumper truck pumps the water while the tanker goes to get more.

GARBAGE TRUCKS

When you put your trash out to be picked up, these big trucks take it away to the landfill.

FRONT LOADER GARBAGE TRUCK

This type of garbage truck has forks at the front that slide into slots on the side of a dumpster and lift the container over the top of the truck, flipping it upside down so the contents dump into the truck.

GRAPPLE GARBAGE TRUCK

Workers use grapple trucks to collect bulky waste or brush. A large claw on the end of a boom crane grasps the bulky item and then places it in the truck's trailer so it can be carried away.

REAR LOADER GARBAGE TRUCK

A worker can empty garbage cans into the open back of this type of garbage truck. Then a compacting blade inside the truck smashes the garbage to make room for more.

GLASS RACK TRUCK

These trucks have special racks built on their sides to protect fragile panes of glass that are being moved from one place to another.

H

HAY LOADER

A hay loader is a tractor with a special forked attachment on the front. Farmers use it to load large bales of hay onto the hay truck.

HAY TRUCK

This semitractor-trailer is a flatbed truck that carries bales of hay. Large hay trucks can hold more than 25 tons (22.7 tonnes) of hay per load.

HIGHWAY PAINT STRIPER

Have you ever wondered how the lines on roads and highways are so straight? A paint striper is a truck built to paint the stripes on roads and highways. Some models can carry more than 2,000 gallons (7,571 l) of paint.

ICE-CREAM TRUCK

These trucks have specially built freezers in the back to store ice cream. Most ice-cream trucks play music to let people know they are in the neighborhood.

IMPACT HAMMER

Impact hammers are used to break rock into smaller chunks. Attach one to a loader or an excavator and it becomes an impact hammer vehicle.

J

JINGLE TRUCK

Called jingle trucks because of the metal chains and chimes hanging from the front bumpers, these elaborately decorated and colorful trucks can be found throughout central Asia in countries such as India, Afghanistan, and Pakistan. They are used to haul many types of goods and cargo.

K

KNUCKLE BOOM TRUCK

A knuckle boom is a type of crane that bends in the middle, like a finger at the knuckle. Attached behind the cab, these cranes load and unload material from the truck. Knuckle booms have a long reach and can move around and over obstacles.

LOADERS

These types of tractors are fitted with tools, usually a scoop, on the front and are used to move loose material, such as dirt, sand, rocks, or snow.

FRONT END LOADER

The wide bucket connected to the front of the truck scoops up material from the ground. Then the bucket lifts up and tips back so nothing falls out while it moves the load. When the truck gets where it's going, the bucket tilts down to dump the load.

GIANT WHEEL LOADER

This giant earthmover can scoop a large amount of dirt and rocks, about 80 tons (73 tonnes) per load. It is designed to fill the biggest trucks as fast as possible.

SKID LOADER

This more compact loader is used for smaller jobs, and it can have many different tools attached to its front. The loader can be used to move bark, plow snow, or make ramps for larger trucks.

TRACK LOADER

This type of loader is used for many of the same jobs as other loaders, but it moves on tracks instead of wheels.

LOG FELLER or HARVESTER

This machine can cut a tree at its base with a powerful saw while holding it with a grapple, or claw. After the tree is cut, the feller carries the log away.

LOGGING TRUCK

A logging truck is a flatbed semitrailer fitted with poles along the sides to hold logs. Strong chains are used to keep the logs in place.

LOWBOY

This flatbed semitrailer is built much lower to the ground than a regular flatbed. Lowboys are often used to move large vehicles because the vehicles can be driven right onto the trailer.

LUNCH TRUCK

Sort of like a restaurant on wheels, this special type of delivery truck is outfitted to cook and serve lunch food. These trucks can be found near office buildings, construction sites, college campuses, warehouses, and other places where people work, live, and shop.

MONSTER TRUCK

Monster trucks are pickup trucks that have supersized wheels—their enormous tires stand almost 6 feet (1.8 m) tall. These giant machines crush old cars, make daring leaps over obstacles, and race one another through mud to entertain fans in stadiums.

M

MAIL TRUCK

A delivery truck is used to deliver the mail. The current custom-designed mail truck can carry up to 1,000 pounds (454 kg) of mail.

MOBILE HOME MOVING TRUCK

This powerful semitrailer is a type of oversized load truck specially equipped to carry an entire house from one place to another.

MOVING TRUCK

This semitrailer carries people's possessions from one place to another when they move to a new house. Most moving trucks are lined on the inside with quilted fabric to help protect furniture and other belongings.

N

NATURAL GAS TRUCK

Trucks of all sizes can be outfitted with engines that use alternative fuels, such as natural gas. Natural gas is a cleaner alternative to the diesel fuel used by most trucks.

NEWS TRUCK

Television news journalists use these trucks to report breaking news from different places. Most news trucks have satellites and other equipment that help reporters broadcast the news on location.

OFF-ROAD PICKUP

This truck, used in Antarctica and other snowy places, is fitted with tracks instead of tires to help it navigate heavy snow and areas with deep cracks in the ice.

OVERSIZE-LOAD TRUCK

An oversize load is heavier than the loads usually allowed on public roads. Most semitrailers that carry oversize loads travel with two smaller trucks, one that drives in front of the load and one that drives behind it. These trucks warn other drivers and help keep the roads safe while the oversize load is passing.

P

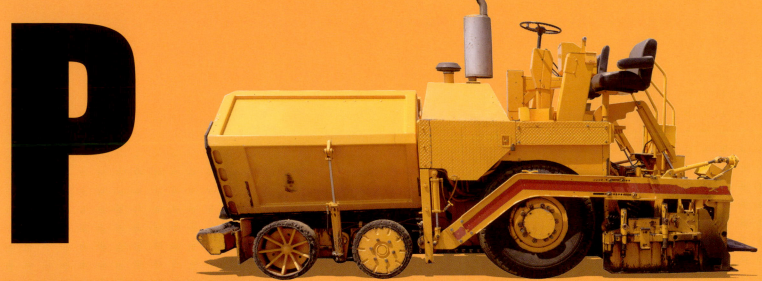

PAVER FINISHER

This vehicle lays down the final coat on asphalt and concrete roads to make them flat and smooth for people to drive on.

PICKUP

Pickups can be light and compact or heavy enough to carry or pull large loads, but they all have an open bed in the back. The first pickups were sold in the 1920s, and these trucks continue to be popular today.

PIGGYBACK TRUCK

This truck can move several tractors, or the front part of a semi, at once by hooking them together, one on top of another—piggyback style.

PILE DRIVER

This machine pounds piles—long poles made of wood, steel, or reinforced concrete—deep into the ground. The piles are used to support bridges or to construct foundations for buildings.

POLICE TRUCK

Police trucks are used in areas where roads are rough or when police may need to patrol off-road areas.

PUSHBACK TRACTOR

This tractor, also called a tug, works at an airport, where it helps guide planes away from the gate before takeoff. Built low to the ground to fit under the nose of a plane, these tractors are heavy and have motors powerful enough to pull huge airplanes.

Q

730E

QUARRY TRUCK

These massive trucks used in mining
are built to carry loads of up to 75 tons
(68 tonnes) of rocks and stones.

R

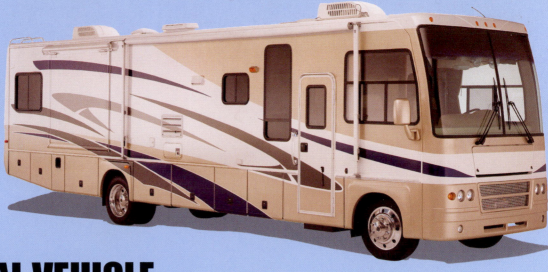

RECREATIONAL VEHICLE

A large recreational vehicle, called an RV for short, is a type of bus with a powerful diesel engine. Some people live in their RVs, which can be furnished like homes, while others use them for vacation travel.

RECYCLING TRUCK

These trucks collect recyclable materials, such as glass, cans, paper, and some plastics, and take them to stations to be sorted, cleaned, and eventually reused to make new things.

REFRIGERATOR TRUCK

Designed to travel long distances with foods, medicines, or other goods that spoil at warm temperatures, these semitrucks have cooling systems built into the trailers. Trucks that carry a separate refrigeration unit, or box, are called reefers. These trucks can transfer their reefer to a cargo ship.

ROAD GRADER

As part of a team of vehicles used to make a road, this machine smoothes out the surface after a bulldozer has cleared it. The long blade that hangs between the two sets of wheels is dragged along the ground to make a flat, smooth surface.

ROAD ROLLER

This heavy machine rolls over the surface of a road to press it down and give it a smooth finish.

ROAD TRAIN

A road train is a superpowerful semitractor that pulls two or more trailers. In remote parts of the United States, Canada, Mexico, and Australia, these vehicles transport large, heavy loads. Some road trains have up to six trailers attached. The world record is held by a road train in Australia that had 114 trailers!

S

SAND TRUCK

This special truck is made to glide over sand dunes, or giant hills of sand. It has large rear wheels called paddle tires that give the truck traction in the loose, soft sand.

SCIENCE SUPPORT VEHICLE

Built for the harsh conditions of Antarctica, this six-wheeled truck can bust through ice and is used to transport science equipment for special expeditions. The truck is equipped with solar panels for an extra power supply.

SCISSOR TRUCK

The scissor truck is a type of semitrailer with a platform on it that can be lifted straight up into the air. The platform is attached to linked supports that open when it goes up and close when it comes down, like the blades on scissors.

SEMI TRUCK

Also called tractor-trailers, semis, and eighteen-wheelers, these big rigs have 18 wheels and carry goods on highways. They have two parts: the tractor, where the driver cabin and engine are, and the trailer, where the load is carried. The device that connects the two is called a fifth wheel and lets the truck bend as it moves around corners.

SKIDDERS

These trucks are used to pull cut trees out of a forest after they have been logged.

CABLE SKIDDER

This type of skidder uses a long metal cable to grab the cut trees and a crank to pull the trees out of the forest. Then the skidder drags the load to the landing area.

GRAPPLE SKIDDER

A grapple skidder has a claw attached to the tractor that picks up logs and carries them to a landing area, where they'll be loaded onto a logging truck.

SNOW BLOWER

Used to remove snow from roadways, this truck has blades on the front for breaking up the snow. A vacuum in the truck sucks up the snow and blows it over a bank to clear the area.

SNOW PLOW

This heavy-duty truck pushes an 8- to 10-foot (2.4- to 3-m) blade through snow and ice to clear the streets after a big snowfall. A plow also may be attached to the front of a tracked loader.

STAIR TRUCK

These trucks are used on airport runways to help passengers safely get on or off an airplane. The back of the truck has a staircase that can extend up to 20 feet (6.1 m) into the air to reach the doors of large planes.

STAKE-BED TRUCK

The stake-bed refers to a cage of posts built onto the flatbed of a truck to help hold materials in place. Stake-bed trucks can be pickups or semitractor-trailers.

STREET SWEEPER

These large, slow-moving trucks help keep streets clean. The revolving brushes attached to the front and underside of the truck sweep garbage and litter from city streets into a path. The litter is then vacuumed into a storage container in the truck.

T

TANKER TRUCK

This type of semi has a large, usually cylinder-shaped, tank to carry liquids such as milk, oil, or gasoline.

TELESCOPIC HANDLER

This truck combines the work of a loader, crane, and forklift into one. Its telescopic boom with a forklike attachment extends up to 30–40 feet (9–12 m) into the air to reach loads too high for other forklifts. It can then place those loads in hard-to-reach places like the top of a roof.

TERRA BUS

The terra bus moves people around the polar bases of Antarctica. It is really more of a powerful bus than a truck, and there are said to be only 10 in existence.

TOW TRUCKS

These special trucks are equipped to lift and move wrecked or disabled vehicles.

CAR TOW TRUCK

Tow trucks move broken-down cars from one place to another or pull out cars that have gotten stuck in snow or mud. Sometimes called wreckers, these trucks use pulleys, chains, and hooks attached to the back to lift the front wheels of a car off the ground. The rear wheels of the car remain on the road as it is being towed.

HEAVY RECOVERY TOW TRUCK

Like a tow truck for cars, this large semi pulls other big trucks that have broken down or need help out of hazardous situations.

TRENCHERS

These heavy-duty machines are used to cut or dig long ditches in the ground.

CONCRETE CUTTER

A concrete cutter is a type of trencher used to cut through streets for repair or to widen a road. The large-toothed cutting wheel on the back of the vehicle slices right through concrete.

ROCKWHEEL TRENCHER

A rockwheel is a type of trencher fitted with a huge, strong blade that can cut through rock and hard-packed earth to dig a trench.

TRACK TRENCHER

This trencher has a rotating chain that digs straight, narrow trenches for laying electrical, cable, and telephone lines as well as pipes for water and gas.

UTILITY TRUCK

Electricians, carpenters, contractors, and others use these trucks to keep their tools safe and organized. Most utility trucks have storage boxes, racks, and other useful features.

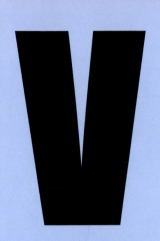

VACUUM TRUCK

This truck, similar to an excavator with its long hose attached, sucks up water, dirt, dust, and other debris into the tank on the back like a giant vacuum.

WHEELIE TRUCK

These trucks are built to entertain. They are designed from the inside out to rise up on their hind wheels, and then roll and turn in circles. Wheelie trucks have a big engine in the back instead of the front, which gives the back of the truck weight and power.

X

X-RAY TRUCK

Designed with X-ray equipment on board, this truck screens cargo containers at airports and seaports to make sure nothing illegal is brought into a country.

Y

YARD SPOTTER

This half-sized cab truck works in ports, truck terminals, and railroad yards to move cargo-loaded trailers. The small cab gives the drivers a clear view of where they are going.

Z

ZAMBONI

First built in 1949 by Frank Zamboni, this special machine quickly resurfaces ice at skating rinks and hockey arenas. A blade shaves the surface of the ice. Then water is spilled onto the ice and mopped up. Finally, clean, hot water is spread on the ice to create a perfectly smooth surface. The Zamboni travels at about 10 miles per hour (16 kph) and weighs more than 5,000 pounds (2,268 kg).